To all the Barnabys.
all the Best.
- Father Leo.
June 1981.

# *Irish Portraits and other poems*

# Irish Portraits and other poems

Leo R. Ward

Fides/Claretian
Notre Dame, Indiana 46556

*Photos on cover, page 1, and page 45 by Vernon Sigl*

**Library of Congress Cataloging in Publication Data**

Ward, Leo Richard, 1893–
Irish portraits and other poems.

1. Ireland—Social life and customs—Poetry.
I. Title.
PS3545.A679I7 811′.5′4 78-10883
ISBN 0-8190-0629-7

## About These Poems

The poems in "Irish Portraits" are an attempt to say how Irish men and women appeared to me, how they spoke and how they took life, joy and pain, during the several seasons they tolerated me among them. The poems are a spin-off from many happy experiences and to some degree from my books, *God in an Irish Kitchen* and *All Over God's Irish Heaven*.

The second set of poems speaks, though by no overall design, on quite current interests, recycling, population, pressure advertising, abortion, the absurd, the "who am I" syndrome and mystery, walking on the moon, and being in the world. Philosophers would say that these poems are existential. They have come to me one by one and are recorded with no concerted idea of remaking the world. A flock of Irish peasant poets in the olden days was said by one of their group to be "making songs of all that would be happening," and shouldn't later scribblers fall in line with their fellow travelers of a thousand years ago?

"Walking on the Moon" won the Laus tibi Deo poetry award for 1970, and "Only Once" won the Catholic Press Association poetry award for 1971. A few of the poems in the second part have appeared— in the *Boston Pilot,* the *Critic,* the *Ligourian,* the *New York Times, U.S. Catholic,* and *Way,* and some from the first part appeared in *Juggler:* many thanks to the esteemed editors. My friends, Thomas and Alberta White of St. Louis, have graciously helped to see the poems through the press.

L.R.W.

# *Contents*

## *Part One:* **Irish Portraits**

## *Part Two:* **No God An Island**

# *Part One:* **Irish Portraits**

## Ever and Always

When did I write these verses?
God help us, did I? Think Irish now

It was Ever and Always
in the depths of my mother's womb
before I was begotten at all
it was nature saying what to say.
More than my own soul
it was the nostalgic thing
from endless ages echoing,
it was the bog, the mountains,
the race compounded making evident
glamorous shining objects
richly humanized events
that, inspected by other minds, might
evaporate like morning dew

God and his saints
be in my heart and on my lips
as I think to give language
to men and women whose
everyday talk is an art

*This poem appeared in* Juggler, *Fall 1975*

## Hitchhiker

You're walking it alone by yourself?

BUSES STOP HERE

They do, but that man you see
There boarding his car

Sir, are you by any chance for Dublin?
'Deed we will and you're a grand creature

Give us this day, Holy Mary
Now and at the hour of our —
These motor cars, perilous to life and limb
Always chasing after like dogs set on cats
Every bone in your body
Often as not I do see corpses
Piled in stacks by the roadside
God help us, I hope well prepared
Every soul of them—slow
Would you! That lorry!
Give me my two good legs
Under me to walk it afoot any day

Stop here now, my man,
Let me go free out of this
To my well earned peace and quiet
And God save me once again
No squawking horn tied to me
In Dublin's fair city
A demure Mollie Malone

Juggler, *Fall 1975*

## Dublin Arena

Flashing flags of six nations
blacks, bays and greys
sashaying, pacing, le'pping,
    horseflesh first,
    men and women capitulating,
    lives and times shaped
    to the horse's hoofs and withers
    to what he will or he won't

    Cork pottery
    Waterford glassware
    Irish sugar. Irish woollens
"What will the Common Market do to your product?"
"Why did you choose Ireland for your holiday?"
Irishmen would know: Yank
pilgrims did not choose Ireland,
it was Ireland chose them
before ever the Horse Show was

"Here, right here, take this seat."
Seraphim, legions of them, sang it
Irish angels, glory to God, echoed it
St. Patrick said a word or two
crowding non-Gael intruders out.
Alongside with depth of nature
to Ireland and horses a man
who had tramped the deough[1] of the curragh,
into his book goes each horse's story
and the man's ecstacy into mine

[1]"Deough," grassy plains

"That horse, bred and born in Brazil,
those Italian horses, they're pure Irish
a fine leap—oh, oh, lightly!
Go lightly, my man!
Watch: that horse knows this arena,
the hedge and water all measured
        Great jump, that!
        No shadow left over,
        a neck on him
        substance to that horse
        nice, short-coupled
        tidy as a pin
That girl's horse—watch—will make
heavy weather of this bank
Oh, oh, God! The horse won't have it,
hopeless, out of the show.

"Rose Mary Robinson! The best till last.
Is she good? Champion of all Ireland,
rode point-to-point last winter
born horsewoman, sister of Willie"

## Riders at the Sea

Straying to us like a dog
the skeleton of a man
unless it's how he maybe chanced
to pull in here for the races.
Ah, some one will harbor his weariness
they will sure, 'twould be
the devil's own town would
leave an old cripple to perish
dead or alive in the street

Cozied up for himself on stone
before some one's open fire
a drop of something in him
        the talk of the town
        himself and the races

Short, fat little barrels
        empties set in squares
        canvas to cover them
        a canteen this day
to dispense rounds of ale and porter
"Ah, sure, a tune-up, and maybe
it's never again a day!"

Sthreeleens of people coming
        jolty side-cars and traps
        faithful nags in a trot
        families sore-footing the miles,
        a mere bit of a thing this day

"That air, it's a good strong air!
Ach! By the sea, what else?"

"You're improved, John, in your person
you, you're grosser-looking"

"Thank God for it, I'm well and I
hope all in your keeping
are as hearty as any fish in the sea"

"That's Joyce's mare, the pure black
coming from beyond the mountain."

"Thrue for you, girleen, Joyce's mare
she's jet black, but a stripe in her face
any man would know Joyce's"

Sand wet and firm good to run on,
hoof-cups of it tossed white into the air

"That's a tidy little race!
A strong mare, the grey, and kind
as kind she is as a child.
Strong, too, and it stood to her"

"The missus herself, didn't I see her
below, it's hers making the turn.
I'm delighted for her, the way
she can do with the winnings"

Men, women, children a heterogeneity
this day between heaven and earth
the Atlantic lapping unnoticed at their feet

## What's that you say?

—1—

A Yank woman came one summer
up high on a horse for herself
she was and didn't she put
the children's words what they'd say
back to them through some rigging she had
but little Margy below said
it didn't half sound like it would be
her own voice talking at all
and they everyone mostly said
it was far too creepy for fun

—2—

The way it would be before you knew it
that's how he said it would be in Ireland
I said 'twould not ever, men nor the priests
won't let it here. He said a soldier
from where I forget where he said
everything there and people gone to the dogs
women with scarce a stitch to their loins
and men as bad in bare-legged tights.
I said foreigners and the likes of them.

—3—

I wonder does it run by itself
the way a cat would or maybe a fish?
They have to learn it early
like how to fiddle or butcher a beef
the ins and outs and ups and downs
ten fingers all the time going
on my life it's a trade in itself
making the words like you'd see on a book

## Nature in them

(*The ghost to Hamlet: "If you have any nature in you, avenge your father's death."*)

Sure now they do, they have nature.
It's in them. Our dog Rex,
I tell you it's a caution
the way they do, that lad
feels it in the air who are
his friends in this house and any neighbor's

Again off with herself
dozing by the kitchen stove,
the head jerking up again
bouncing like a ball.
Couldn't the two of us do
with maybe another cup of tea?

Look at him now, an itch or tickle
on him, he'll flick his back—
see that!—What was it I was saying?
Oh, 'twas the depth the nature
runs in them, it's how from
little pups it gets into them
like an extra ear or heart

They're coming from the field now,
look, his ears pop sharp up
and a bit of whinny—Hello there!—
to his talk, the tail thumping,
nature sure as God breaking out of him

## Galway Bay

Water lying still as a pond
gold and brick and umber
the dying sun glamorous over Galway Bay

Against the sea, green fields
littered with browsing sheep
the fields greener
the sheep whiter
after the long day's rain

Tops of houses sending up
blue-grey turf smoke
people turning their minds to tea
a girl on a bicycle herding
two black cows home for the milking,
shepherdess as content as her cows
facing the salute to Bay and sky

## The Claddagh*
*For Eamon de Valera, "Up Dev!"*

Lonesome you be these days for the huts
in olden times at the Claddagh
your dead-and-gone home sweet home
it's Boston and the likes makes anyone
double his heart back and it sick
for the way the Claddagh once would be
God spare us, its walls sagging
pots and pans to catch the drip
babies stored in any corner
home it was, home sweet home

Many's the good man and woman
lived in them, died quick in them, too
only God while He did kept souls stitched up
and the bite of potato to our plate
home wasn't it, a dear sweet home

Dev put a roof over Ireland
slate between Claddagh and the sky
a warm dry bed to sleep on,
the fish, though, yet wary of our bait
in the troughs and furrows of the sea
ourselves under the hard
and miserable mercy of the world
a penny or two for our trouble
and the pittance allowed for being poor

**The Claddagh, meaning seashore, is a group of families, mostly fishermen, at the edge of Galway City.*

## So Damn Contrary*

Lines of people knee-walking,
lines hunching their way
across the rocky top of a hill,
a dozen as if crucified
against the wall of the church

What are we into this for
but to do his purgatory the way he did,
Lord pity our bodies
and bones turned inside out
and didn't I ever my best day
hate their blasted black tea
and that oaten bread God save us
it's like the granite beside the road

Musha, now, he did it, Porrig himself
started this, ages on ages it was gone by,
three days it wasn't at all
but longer much than half your life,
round and round, pillar to post,
in his feet and them bleeding,
The little we do, it's not up to here on him.
Patrick and Brigit, Columkill and Killian see us
awake and alive this night through.

Ages gone into the past that was—
the taste of that dry oat bread,
the sharp crust stuck in my throat
and under me the feet burning like sods of turf!

**People are doing penances at Lock Derg*
*in County Donegal all summer long.*

Arra, look at them, some hereabouts
can't they skip like lambs of the flock
nor hill nor dale a hurdle to them.
That hunchback mound of a hill
looked straight in the face
at midnight, the moon breaking through,
ain't it a little thing, to be so damn contrary!

Wishwashy grey hair in her face,
what is she doing in it,
making her purgatory twice in the one summer!
Maybe it's to catch a bride for her son?
"If it was, itself!"
Eligible girls here in plenty.
"The priest's match is unlucky!"

Toughest of all would you say
is it six to ten, mornings, or is it
the depth of the night? One hour
as hard as another, only maybe a little harder
but the Almighty God our witness,
the Canon's droning is the hardest,
little wonder he said (Luke was it, or John?):
"I clothed myself with a hairshirt"

## At Home on the Road

Long dusk of the June evening
Night held waiting in the sky
A clan-like family, the day's foraging done,
at home on the road
    the fire alive on a face or two,
    desultory chitchat
    hobbled ponies munching
Where if anywhere the next day's work,
when if ever a day of school?
Foolish greenhorn questions
beyond sense or answer
in the tinkers' roving paradise

Tinkers, they're gypsies, aren't they?
Gypsies they are not, they're tinkers.
How can you tell? Gypsies will steal,
Tinkers, they maybe might take
some things but tinkers won't steal

Out with them, I say! Into the North Sea.
They're a burden and a disgrace.

Ah, man! The freedom they love is Irish,
any one of them as Irish as the next man
to their bones and gizzards. They couldn't pay
in chickens and pigs, and to
the side of the road "distressingly" the poet said,
    their hovels levelled,
    families with God alone over them
    from that day to this
    it was catch as catch can

Long-haired little Willie, a blond
all dressed up, a fine new suit on him
and to remain on him day and night
until Willie wears it off.
Happy in his learning, did he not
go to the convent to be put through
the ABC's of faith, hope and charity
and fall heir to God in the Eucharist?

"When will you go to school, Willie?"
"I went to school"

Willie's mama in the street,
some one's baby crooked in her arm,
hand ready toward any overture.
"How's little Willie?" "Oh, Willie!
He's cracked alive about you,
I think he'll be a priest!
Cuculain Street is it you're looking for?
I'll take that bit of a step with you.
There, now! And God be with you going"

I cannot send greetings to a boy
who has no address and cannot read,
but is it greetings that Willie
or the likes of him wants for Christmas?

On the open plains of Kildare,
the sweet grass nibbled by champions,
lived Auntie Mae, first a crippled girl
and long a crippled woman.
On May day friends handed her,
of all things, a dress flaming red,

a bit of finery never to touch
Mae's drooping shoulders.
A tinker girl knocked one day,
smiling ready to take a man,
from that day the dress hung
flamingly on the lucky girl
        before the altar
        before open fires in June
        begging in the street
        a baby on her arm

## Keatie

She turned then, just a wispeen of a girl
to go back alone at midnight
the sky over her
the sea and mountains around her
and what she went back to was the house
raised a few feet above the bog
where she had everything
in her simple, bloodless little hand

Juggler, *Fall 1975*

## The Fire does Burn

(A dozen in the kitchen, the only light coming from the open fire, everybody, anybody speaking in any order, irregular silences punctuated by sighs)

It's a wonder, surely to God now
it is a wonder himself
wouldn't see to a good day (*silence*)

A wonder of the world

Come in, Penny, always welcome to a man and his dog

God be praised, we'll squat right here

Rain or shine, The Day the Reek*
Ah, sure, whatever, they'll be climbing,
any weight of them
and they everyone in their feet

Thousands. They will. Can't you
see them in your eye, twisty
patches of them like geese and ducks
out of Dublin and Cork gabbling,
and beyond from the Arans
and the North even,
God between us and all harm

How many years is it, God save us,
and we never once saw the sun
on The Day the Reek?

**The Reek is Croagh Patrick, Saint Patrick's own mountain in County Mayo; the last Sunday of July is The Day the Reek, the day of an annual pilgrimage.*

Long (*sighed*). It's that long you wouldn't
remember the half of it. Maybe you
do, Pat, you're a man far up

Old times gone I do, I do well
recollect once a day, was it forty years past,
a Day the Reek and the sun shining
hot, blazing through any coat you wore

Not a good sign, that,
not for The Day the Reek

It won't be likely such a day
seen twice in any man's life
but they say old times do
unravel and come back again
(*silence and a sigh or two*)

There's no changing the times,
but there'll be crowds by our leave or no.
Nor would we, not one of us.
Times are as good one way as another

Forty days and forty nights
and the chill and freeze of it
seeping into every crevice and cranny
of your bones, God save Ireland!

Not a chill nor a chill
did people feel in the olden days,
that's the God's honest truth

Ach, sure! The old people in them times!
Devil a cold nor a cold
did they take from it, a one of them,
and the icy wind torrentious

He stood the whole time, his arms up
I don't know did he (*silence*)

'Tis shocking to think. 'Twas hard,
left to himself a man couldn't, no man,
praying God all the day and the night long
(*a sigh; silence; a sigh*)

He wouldn't come down and
he wouldn't, not a foot nor a foot

Till, Mick, he wouldn't till
he got the Promises ratified,
deadly set Patrick was on the Promises

The snow and ice on that Mountain
and the Saint in his feet
and maybe no cloak to his back!

Put on a sod of turf, Maggie:
these nights do be down-draughty

Ever and ever exacting the Promises,
the Faith never to quiver nor quake

to falter never, whatever

In Ireland! It won't!

It cannot! It's one of the Promises,
the Lord's word stands firm forever (*silence*)

(*in a deep sigh*) Like a rock.
Wonderful it was, ever and always
he kept faced the one way toward the Morning Star

He did? Well, these ears never till this day heard that

Nor mine as much and by gor I wonder
There's no word of it in the Promises and don't
the child from this high know every word of them?

Up there the best day ever, if it's
a breath it's a storm,
man nor beast can stand it,
a storm and it pouring
in out of the ocean pellmel on him

Headfirst didn't it come dreadful on him
tumbling in across Clew Bay
'twas worse they say in the old days,
one year or another wasn't it
for all the world like
the night of the Great Wind?
You remember that, yourself?

Was it, I don't know, a reprimand,
that Wind? Can any man tell was it
before or after the Promises?

Before or after, God knows.
That Wind, old people used to say,
tore the skin off a man's back
and he riding a white horse

Glory be to God!

Another record tells that the horse
was skinned to the hooves of his feet.
It blew turnips out of the ground

Forty days

And forty nights,
the mercy of the world on us!
Who'd be able for it now
in these our latter days?

The man stood his ground, one installment
and another till the list was full

This strange thing, too, any dirt
your clothes collect The Day the Reek
they say it's gone clean swept the morrow

Arra now is it so slick gone,
a new kind of detergent
(*silence, and a sigh*)

We've seen greater. Women up to eighty—

and some of them well long past—

climbing that rocky slope on
their bare knees like kittens.
Nine lives some of them do possess (*silence*)

Do you think will Father Angellus be in it?

Why wouldn't he, that man? What's to let him?
Sure, now, as sure as The Reek is there
and he up it through storm and stress
maybe it's like these twenty years—

Twenty is it! If it's half that
it's up another decade or two
and starting yet another. God knows
I've seen him there unsheltered
on that Mountain black in his face
from the cold, his beard flowing
and flapping like it would catch fire
from the wick on the altar candles,
and would that man desist before
the Mass was terminated and the
Faithful waiting on his words
(*breathing can be heard and a sigh or two*)

They say the fire does always—

## Man of Aran

Withereen of a woman, and she dark Irish,
daring to throw words of wisdom at
the Man of Aran.
"Happier" shook out of her,
"happier, that's why you always came back,
people are happier here"

"Woman," smoothly spun out of him,
then "Woman" on a turned-up note,
"you wouldn't know where you'd be happier,
you nor I, on God's earth where.
Look at the specimen before you
here today and gone tomorrow
and the church bells of Aran
won't ring their tongues out
saying Goodbye to Stephen"

"Take care, though, would you fall—
God spare us—over that rock
and it straight down to the sea!"

"Ever and forever down. An' sure did I fall
how much loss or gain to the world?
A little space cleared for another
and what do I bequeath to a hungry world?
this, my old tripod hat
my two turned-up shoes
and a hole on one of them

"Rock! Rock! Don't blast our rock,
a commodity we have in plenty,
it's the one only wall between us
and the bottom of that pond,
Woman, I'm telling you"

## Erin go Brach

Windswept soul along the sea,
the slapping surf swept over him,
hungry belly, torso improvisedly covered,
reddened face, draggy steps his transport
from bog to rock and back again,
only by an effort God knows
are his tattered body and mystic soul
kept close together

A slave surely, believing
himself sprung from kings,
full of lofty ideas and kept
to the wet sunless earth

## The High Cross of Tuam*

The world keeps the dust swirling
round the High Cross of Tuam
on this day of the Fair and *Flead Ceoil.*[1]
A fat woman comfy on a box
peddling her fries and hens,
"potatoes quick cleared out, too"
A disheartened huckster:
"It's dancing they want, not saddles and bridles"
Tinkers densely populating
a corner. "Ach! is it pennies
the best the Yanks can do!"
Thick planks on strong posts,
children dancing "The Three-Cornered Cap"

The Angelus: traffic and talk stayed,
then as if on a leash free moving.
A man tailing a lean cow,
a wedding party, its young and old
without gap in stride, a funeral
solemnly circling the Cross,
men with hats tilted at their breasts
all parties crossing themselves

Alas and again alas for lovely
off-limits St. Mary's below
temporarily held by the enemy,[2].

**King Torlough O'Connor and Abbot Aeth O'Hoison erected this Celtic Cross in the 12th century at Tuam, County Galway.*

[1]The Fair is a market, the Flead Ceoil (Kuhl) is a community celebration featuring contests in native songs and dances.

[2]Since the 16th century

only an exotic straggler or two
chancing to open its panoplied door
after missing the universal way
where King O'Connor and Priest O'Hoison
marked a path for man
round the High Cross of Tuam

## Man about town

***(Salute to Mr. M. J. Devine, dramatist and actor)***

Ah, many times, many plays I did,
back twenty years gone by it was,
a small book of them. We played a few.
My father set us drama-playing,
brought drama alive, my own teacher
that man, teacher of the village.
The Canon, oh, didn't he have fits
and worse: said drama-playing
would be the ruin of many in Tubercurry,
then the self-same adamant Canon
came down from his tower and led the march

True, true this Sligo town
is convenient to Yeats country
but independent as Ireland itself

Oh, long, long ago, many parts

Right! We never got over it
the town reborn through drama,
all kinds made into one.
You know—maybe you don't—
in Irish life there's some "big feeling,"
Goodbye to that, knocked into a cocked hat.
Top-dog "big people" weren't the top rung
to act a part; for years on years
our best was the town's tailor
from he was twenty till near sixty.
Another thing, people grew up,
a lot of them, in how to value
and evaluate, to know right roles and costumes.
An old woman from a farm
showed us a girl's regalia was wrong
and our best judge of final showing,
the Dublin critic said, was the cobbler

Oh, we did, we chose great plays
from Lady Gregory, Louis D'Alton,
Paul Vincent Carroll, and *Isogan*
by Padraic Pearse, played in Irish
one night and in English the next

## On Time

Straggler woman to woman:
"It's not off again with you?"
"I am, this minute, for a loaf of bread"
her pace leisurely criss-crossing the street,
plenty of God's good time and she knew it,
"past time, on time" in the land of saints and scholars!

"Where's this Mrs. Fitzsimons
herself and that creamy, dreamy
niece she totes along with her?
A nice maneuver to leave us stranded,
aint it now, waiting"

"Joe, would you be kind, dear,
holding up for just a minute like?"

"I will, ma'am, and willing
and you get a shake on you.
For God's sake now is it into
the hair-doer's she's turning?
And look, would you, at the look
of the hat on her head:
What color of a hat now
would you say it is?
Paycock blue I'd almost say,
it's that grand on her the heart
can it stay planted in any man's breast?"

"We're rollin' now, ah, we are,
a wee bit of a mile it is, once you descend,
or maybe it's about two at the most"

"Troth then it's five if it's one. Don't get off yet!"

"Walked it I did, peg-leg and all, and I'd say
it's maybe like three or wouldn't you say four"

"Never fear, the road will be there ahead of you"

"Keep to your right, it's mostly on your right"

"Faith, then, 'tisn't. It's more to your left,
Keep left, and God be with you. Poor man"

## Mrs. Mack's Boxtie

Grey-green patties overflowing the plate
to caress her fat, indelicate fingers
"Boxtie! How are you for a round of boxtie?
With your tea you'll love it!
One bite and—careful! it's hot! Now!"

The trouble with her, the heart's grown
too big to be shut up in a compartment
called a person; it's like the off-shore island
that bred her, only a continent or a nation could house it

"Would you want, the three of you's,
I'd put the bottle in, these cold July nights,
You know I could easy for every one"

Boxtie or no goose-grey boxtie,
the bottle or rolling into icy sheets,
great is the Lord that made her,
great and greatly to be praised,
herself buxom and generous
made in the image of God

## Kings

Are you a king, then?

I am. Deep in my bosom rings a bell
saying Irishmen are of kingly stature
"the noble drop in them."
Let the bedraggled wanderer
be received at the hearth,
the house spacious and grand enough,
itself a king's palace,
the lot of us sprung
from kings of bygone ages

Come, sit down for yourself
poor soul destroyed with traveling,
you must be dying for the cup,
when I'm alone estrayed like that
I do be dying for the cup

Ah, sure not yet! Another sip
and you'd not be leaving us already,
aint it a pity! But wait:
we have a law—weren't we
just at the first decade,
mind you, when you set foot at the door
a Hail Mary or two never hurt anyone—
wait and Sheila or Pat will company you
up that brae, you'd be all alone by yourself!

So she walked to the cacumen[1]
of the hill with me
and ever since then
she and her brother and their mother
have been with me as I have tramped
all the roads of Galway
and Connemara and the world

'Twas Nancy spread the riches of Ireland
before me, and a salute to the Hanrahans,
their kettle slung over the fire
and to Eileen and Dan and their flock,
children and pigs and milkbuckets
a constant source of disaster drama.
Herself shocked: a man planted awry:
"Another old fellow buried on that hill
and him standing up, God help us!"
And to the McDonoughs settled
by an expanse of lake water,
the rock road to their house
built by Peter's and Mary's hands,
their only complaint: "You don't have Irish!"

A terrible storm in the West
and it roaring in from the sea
the kettle and the cow
in a race for the honors
the kettle winning first place,
the cow not far behind

[1]John M. Synge heard this Latin word in west Ireland for the peak or top, and memory suggests that I also heard it.

Only then am I god-blest-voyaged
and escorted as a king by a king
to a nest by the tumbling sea

Heartiness spread all over them
himself racing herself to say:
    "If you can ever come again
    if it is a week or three weeks
    or six months itself
    come and stay in our house"

## Man on a Hill

Lord of people, turf and time,
at his command a hill dense with cattle,
the Atlantic disregarded below

"A fine man and a fine farm."
"True, true for you. But 'twas
schlack in him to let the marrying-time
slip him by. Otherwise, he was genuine."

His house climbing a century or two
toward the top of the hill, its look
less of design and contrivance
than of thrown there, drift and debris,
its floors made to go with the hill,
its thatch on thatch resting on scratch,
"the skin of the mountain"[1]

His reverend self of the parish
a man into land and cattle,
stops by for tea and to inquire:
"Would you let loose now or hold?"
The tone a "which-now in one word"

"Hold I would not. Last year
didn't I and lost near two pounds the head
and them shaking with condition.
All weathers it's hard on cattle,
I seen them here on St. John's Day[2]
shivering on the land wholesale"

[1]"Scrath," the top fibrous layer of soil spaded off the bog ("mountain") before the turf is reached.

[2]June 24th

## I am that Man

"A man I knew long years ago,
the present party it was,
a streak in him and indicted to the drink.
He had a mare, fine legs under her,
into the town for himself
and at one quaff up-ending
thirteen jiggers and, no sight nor sign
of home, the man was stretched
on the brae that night, the mare
like dropping a guard over him
still at sunrise tugging his frock"

I am that man and I swore
that day I would never drink
again outside my own home
and I didn't!

Sixty years later, herself providing
and pouring, Peter Jimmie disposes of
a tall glass bottoms-up
his good clear talk improving

"I knew another man, oh the best
little neighbor, good with cattle,
and it was worse with him,
I tell you why: he had more money
and at one taste, all was beyond hope
till the money was at the last penny"

"This land you walk on, I made it—
Good Lord, no, not with a horse,
one step here and the horse goes down—
it's the ass can get in and get out,
half his weight on his back.
A man builds this land inch by inch
and it's never built but always
slipping back into the bog.
Man has to keep lifting it up
for his praties and inniums—[1]
good fried or done with eggs
and good uncooked, oh, Lord, yes—
man and beast must fertile
the soil with kelp brought
in creels from the sea below
in all winter weathers.
You see what kindness the years
have brought out of it"

There stands Peter Jimmie
holding up soil fertiled for the crop,
and beyond, looking down on him,
stands the Mountain, St. Patrick's own.
"These eighty-nine years I'm looking
and never set foot on it."
Sing as you go his recipe:
"Music is great life.
God bless you now
and leave you the health"

[1]Inniums, pronounced "inn-yums," for onions

## Brave Men All*
*Notes on drying up*

-1-

Never no more I said that morning,
I swore I wouldn't and I didn't
—Peter Jimmie Salmon

-2-

Come up here to this altar
come any who are intent to say
"No for life, never no more for life"
any who labor and are burdened
and fall like dead at the door of the pub

"For life, you say, good God!
Life you know is a long time.
I did, I started up, shaking,
an Irishman of our clan in the West
shaking and quaking, afraid
to put God between him and the drink,
I went to wait and I went to leave

"Ten men brave and bold that day
God help us, up to the altar,
where are the other nine?
Many's the time hearty friends would say:
'A drink, Melia, a sip once with us'
and now these thirty years they know
what God and the wife here know:
Ned is off the bottle
Don't the Irish have element enough?"

Juggler, *Fall 1975*

-3-

A man who well knows the way,
most nights crosses the welcoming mat,
the very last man I ever saw
of those in my well beloved Mayo town
where live my friends and people,
himself just making it, stagger to stagger

-4-

In Tipperary Town, the Sunday between rain and shine,
Publican McObie and seven sober-sides
form a second wall to the Obie House,
himself proper, wise and a friend of man.
Who at all could it be, they ask,
a girl begging in the street!

The weather taking up and letting down,
a bit of Irish mist (says Obie)
chasing around in the mountains.
A young man floundering,
slobbering past, held up by the wife,
herself like a child; not an "Oh!"
or an "Ah, God's mercy on us!"
from any nonplussed observer.
Then a rush of men and boys
into Obies: "Its from the football field
they come and the thirst is on them"

-5-

"Is it from there you're coming," said he,
"and did you have the luck to sample
their best poteen? People do tell
it's a great end of Ireland for that commodity."
"Poteen yourself!" said she,
"It's saving the hay we want now
and look, Mick, God love us,
the cows are on the high places
and that's a good sign"

## Come Dance with me

Narrow sticks of legs flaring with the music,
unstarched nuns the envious tutors
backed by grandmas in their kitchens.
Night and day dancing contests
the Irish avocation for old and young,
flashy dudes and stumbling rustics

Dancing and singing all the go:
"It's the collar of Gold:
We put it together ourselves,
and the Chalice of St. Patrick with it
to say in strings and dance
how people then hammered the silver"

Most of all, dancing for fun:
"Come dance with me in Ireland"[1]
youthful hearts ready at the gong
the top of their lives in song and dance

"All the poor learn to dance,
exceedingly fond of the amusement.
A ragged lad without shoes or stockings
leading up a girl in the same trim
for a minuet

love of dancing and music
almost universal in every cabbin
masters travel from cabbin to cabbin
with a piper or blind fiddler,
an absolute system of education"[2]

Aseneth Nicholson, straight puritan blood,
no dancing foot under her:
"So fond are the Irish of music
that in some form or other
they must and will have it"

A peg-legged piper, said she,
holds a child up to dance.
How he asked could people do at all
on a rainy day
without dropping in for a jig?
"It's nature, you see, ma'am,
they'll dance before they can walk."[3]

[1]William Butler Yeats

[2]Arthur Young, *Tour in Ireland* (1776–1779)

[3]Aseneth Nicholson, *The Bible in Ireland* (1844)

## But Anyhow

Where a body first came
their heart gets tangled full of it
like it was heaven let down.

Often wouldn't he say:
        "Anybody knows it's not
        all what it ought to be"
as if he felt doubled up in it,
and I'd maybe arg with him
and him the man of the house.
Inside me I'd say:
        "The sun sprinkling
        through the trees at the window
        a blessed corner of the world
        and the children every one
        but one bright and strong
        God between them and all harm!"

He'd take it up another day:
        "Shut of it at last
        and better so, the stoop in and out
        fit to bash a man's head.
        This new roof"
and he'd make to reach it
        "no drop of rain nor crease
        of wind seeping through,
        God Almighty, a bite
        within with us, a rag
        or two from head to foot,
        this by far it's better"
and he'd tilt like drinking it

Didn't I know, like right from left,
in every word the truth he spoke:
"Better so, it's better by far,"
even if it wasn't himself said it.
But anyhow, the Lord forgive me,
still and all, don't I be thinking
of the dear place we first came

# *Part Two:* **No God An Island**

## On Being in the World

Only a split second ago
I read it as it was: "twenty to,"
as good a time as any to go on
with my being whatever that is
in the world whatever that is becoming
over-all. At that moment, the script ran:
Caesar—wasn't it?—crossing the Rubicon,
on with him in the freakish familiar world
on with me, too, riveted to the world
as the clock to the wall,
on, didn't I say, with my wandering pondering
which is most of whatever it is to be me,
the I-me thing in its ecological setting,
its insolvent involvement,
entanglement, estrangement in the world

"Twenty," I remember that, it's like a record
in a book written down somewhere
in whatever it is to be me
in the world whatever the world
is and is becoming
because the sensible thing characteristic of me
is that time tables work into me
like rings in a tree or rattles in a snake.
Twenty to—to what? Eleven or twelve or what?
As if that matters to me
whatever I am in the world

## The World Aside

Is there some tight-glued when and where
that is all alone and merely itself,
one when and where, the world aside,
I really and clam-cold am?
I am roughly sure as anything in the world
there was a when and where I used to be,
a glamor unending lifelong day
not in the world at all

## Pussyfooters

Exhilarating, confounding
at war with trivia and himself,
tutored for eons and perennial ignoramus
wolf-hungry and easily fed up
bursting out all over and sapped by a flea,
flapping his technological wings against the stars
and unable to keep his nose clean
a one-time turtle, a pre-maggot
approaching the Omega point
scared of his own shadow
cockiness led by a psychiatric hand

Kierkegaard's, Heidegger's, Chekov's absurd
pussyfooted and they knew it
said beleagured Camus
himself just able to lament:
Absurd, absurd, the gods ruled out
man cannot find it in him to lay
uninhibited claim to his majority

## Only Once

The Lord is my shepherd, I shall not want
Associates, good people with money
Ask and you shall receive
Friendly Bob Adams waiting for you
Pressed down and running over
Enriched and filtered as a cigarette should
Neighbor, could you spare us a loaf?
Give your wife Hawaii for Christmas
Suddenly an angelic host
Forgive us our rock and roll bombardment
Praising God and saying
A lot to live, a lot to give
Glory to God in the highest
Hostile enemy action, hawk dogfighting dove
And peace to men of good will
Where's our territorial pound of flesh
Lay up for yourselves treasures
Credit cards honored, charge it
Where neither rust nor moth consumes
You go round only once in life
If you're asked to walk a mile
Fly the friendly skies of United
Bound up his wounds, took care of him
Nobody swings like Ford, nobody
Blessed are the pure of heart
All you ever wanted to know about sex
Swaddling clothes and laid in a manger
Everything a dog needs, all you add is love

*This poem appeared in the* Ligourian, *Feb. 1971.*
*Winner of Catholic Press Association Poetry Award, 1971.*

## That One There

For past three score and ten I have known
the warmth and intimacy that I am I,
about who I am all in all
no one has so far cared to ask

Pete, Charlie, Al, ye pack of pups!
You there, Dick, can't you chase the flies away,
bring in a stick of wood, finger the bawling calves—
numskull, omadthaun!

That's the inside what of me,
the presumed who of me still extant,
a name put on him, he'll be so-and-so,
that one there

Get your 'rithmetic and abc's
everyone quick find out who he is!
Teacher, this livelong rainy day—
and you still don't know who you are!
Better find out, the sensitivity age inquires,
try some tunes, one might turn you on,
you fell and fell, didn't you, and caught yourself
and learnt to walk. Find out who you are

He's the one stumbled over a straw,
it was him or his appended legs,
it's that railfence pile of bones,
that one there, the cadaver

It's great (you say) to be in college
now you know who you are. Quick tell us:
You're Rosie, yes, but if they'd dubbed you Lu or Ann?
Oh, I think I mean I know who I am

Burn 'lectricity right through the night,
find out what the supermen said:
Aristotle, Ptolemy, Shaftesbury, Occam,
Franklin, the exploits of Jesse James.
Blatherskites supreme,
masters of polysyllabic junk
blackguards polluting men's minds—
did any of them know who he was?

Here I am, Lord, but where is here?
If space science could right me on where here is
would I know the who of me or anybody?
Me, I, who—what difference to youth crises,
to wars in Asia, rocks on the moon?

Me here, couldn't I be someone else instead?

## Heresiarch

Robert Moses up to devilry
Said pollution vows panic aimless people
Salvation in a mop or two
And pity for those lacking environmental brooms
Disease carriers all the way from Adam
Enemies of the people and new clean living

All join hands and sing allegiance
Libs and anti-libs, edgy generations
Black and white soul brothers
Crabs on crutches, waifs on the bottle,
All rock and roll in one ecumenical coalition
A monumental Carry Nation
With banners flashing:

Old Dutch cleanse the atmosphere
Outshine Rachel Carson on land and sea
Bad cess to rats and bugs and excess babies
Salvos to the ecological millenium

## Eden Recycled

A new heaven swept and garnished
No Raggedy Ann people in it
Hell, too, gone bourgeois
Gas heat, floors of Persian muff
Smog evanescent, obsolescent
Cars Naderized f.o.b.
Air and water homogenized
Babies phylacterized, no dirt no more
Worms in the woodwork
Ecologized, re-energized
Gully sludge photosynthesized
Into aboriginal apples
No backfire, no bellyache
Planes and planets fun-tumbling
Caught in seas of absorbent cotton
Deluxe kidnappers parlayed
Into finest public servants

*This poem appeared in the* New York Times, *op-ed. Feb. 22, 1975*

## Master Key

Guest 9088, Retirement Home,
Locked in for safe keeping
A wall like granite says:
"This is home: like it!"
Cornered, sealed-up Mama

Never handy with locks and things
Or smart at eventualities
        darning a pair of socks
        flouncing a skirt
        sifting crumbs into a batter
Expert only on family trees
On who came when from where
And the winds that scattered them
From that day on

"Clambering on three's and four's!
Granny, outside in the snow!"
"Outside? Me outside where?
They're all inside with me
Gold in the hills for Johnny
Minnie due any day now
It's like old times how we're
Rounded up to celebrate"

*This poem appeared in the* U.S. Catholic, *August 1975*

## Better'n Nobody

Trampin' the world, fightin' the family traffic
Stashed away now plumb forgot
He-devils, she-devils all around me
Collectors' items, mouldy butt-ends
Myself a discarded dishrag in a pile of rubbish
Alone, alone like that's my name
Nobody to arg it out with, chop to chop
A banged-up photo's better'n nobody from home
For this bug-headed old son of a—
Stop there young fellow, no damn cussin'
A-lookin' at that yellow flower

Wish I'd a-died the day they put me here
Why didn't I die the day they did?

U.S. Catholic, *Oct. 1976.*
*Third place, Catholic Press Association Poetry Award, 1976*

## The King at Prayer

It's I, David, speaking
Listen, O God, lend me your ear
May God shower truth and love
His glory illumine the earth
The heavens melt at his presence
God bombarded by man
God chased to his lair
A national-possession God
King's and people's
Hear us, O God of Jacob
A choice and covenanted people
Sworn to David, your servant
A dynasty established forever

O Lord, avenging God, listen:
Make putty of pretenders
Give it to them hot and heavy
Their gods wood and stone, bulls eating hay
What better for the best of them
Than to go it with us
On the mapped-out road to glory

The King a head-hunter
Eye for an eye, a tooth or two for a tooth
Smash their babies' brains against the rocks
Good guys, bad guys
What option is open to God or David
The two turned tribal
Mighty men in battle

Glorious things are said of you
O City of God!
Babylon, Egypt, Tyre, Ethiopia
To be counted among Zion's children
She the foster mother of all
David singing and dancing says
They will dance as they sing
The universalist song:
"In you all find their home"

When king or serf says God
Ah-ah-ahs the least God-syllable
He utters endemic meanings
With his own time's trivialities
No other speech accessible
To poet or prophet
So help him, God

## Priest Meditating

You can take the nun
    You can take the nun out of the nunnery
    But you can't take the nunnery out of the nun
Me, priest Jones, too—what's that country-soft,
  baby-sweet ditty?
    You can take the priest off the altar—
    Can you though?—tear that blasted collar off his neck.
A bishop turned Yale psychologists loose to have their say:
    Young priests lack a sense of career success,
    Of expectancy—
That's bookish, but by God they caught the stink of the rectory.
I wish I had what I haven't if I was where I ain't—
    Exuberant me, in a rectory!
In the world I'd cut a figure, have to run my chance
  to scratch a living.
    Me, and I am—or am I a priest forever?
I'd have to practice saying:
Unharness me, get these apish vestments,
  this garbish off my back,
And me not used to work, to going it like a man
Where the action is, looking for a job.
    Good God, where's my rubber collar,
    What's that unthing round my neck?
A new heaven and a new earth—did beloved John
  know how to speak of them?

Hands off, I'm not just a man, I'm a priest—
    There we go again, the irremediable power-authority
    Rubbed into me by that pudgy bishop,
    Pudgy and puggy and him puffing.

*This poem appeared in the* Critic, *July–August, 1970*

Me, half a priest, half here, half nowhere
A misfit clerical Christopher Robin,
        I'm not anybody, I'm someone else instead
        Ex-somebody, pre-nobody.
Damn that chancery-office stuff,
Can't I keep loose, can't it let me go it alone?
Damn old man Melchizedek and "you are a priest forever"

I, Adam Jones, sick and tired, career-defeated,
Lashed to a three-cornered crab horny as a hive of devils,
An ancient hidalgo, the chair a part of him,
A two-three-generation gap, an era—
There, he's shuffling to pour a whiskey sour.
I am his boy to do his will—
        What's he to me or I to him?—
To do what he does, to eat and drink out of his hand.
        Give us this day our daily bread,
        Get me out from under.

It's a game, a dead-end evaporated nothing.
Bread and wine—give me a copped-out dose of unbelief.
It's a made-up package, piles and files of laid-on doctrines
Worn thin with thoughtless use,
        Defunct inanities, clerical jobbery

Give me God and love and hope,
Does a woman bring all these along with her lips and body?
Give me people, I want life,
Give me song and joy and maybe a hippie guitar strumming
        Or wouldn't I go it better on a banjo?

I'll be myself, my own man,
        Acolyte and accolade to no one,
        Willed body and soul to the underground,
        Consorting with subterranean free men

Live or die I couldn't care less,
A lapsed priest, they'll say, defrocked, defaulted
Why don't they say desiccated and defecated?

It used to be, ten years—oh, it's a million years ago—
People kept gawk-looking at me,
        Some, damn them, in admiration-adulation
        Some, damn them too, in adjuration,
  spotting my Roman neck
Why can't I go turtle-necked to the altar,
Bill Veeck it openshirted
Or like that Oklahoma padre celebrate in shorts—
        Poor Okie, his grapes of wrath turned sour

Take a second look, squint like an ape, size me up,
You've got me right, I'm an unjubilant half-priest.
The other day a fellow slobbered up to me, "Hi, Pap!"
The kind of fellow he was that's drunk when he's sober.
But bone-dry preachy-looking women used to gaze and feast,
You know the kind in the John F. Kennedy days,
Me a priest forever, but then just out of the shell.
        No (I said) she, that one peering-leering,
        She won't vote for Kennedy, she won't vote for anyone
        She's too mean, gone to seed too long,
Just like me, Mother of God, how long ago!
The oglers' theme today, it knifes me through:
I wonder if, I bet you that bull is chasing a herd of heifers

I tell you meantime it's not much to tell,
My unromantic, de-solemnized storybook,
not so great an exploit.
        "God be with you"—wherefore can't I say it?
        "Glory to God in the highest," "Merry Christmas"—
Terrible God, you've tied my tongue, the once-simple things.
"Unholy"—no, I cannot say that, either

King and rapist David was able to say "I see."
"I see"—is the world as simple as that?
"I see that all fulfillment has its limits"—
Would God let me preach that simple ghost of a thought?
"Life is a trial, a time of trial, full of miseries"—
No, I could not spew that out, it sounds like
  the old man retching.
"There's a good side to everything"—that's him rambling again.
Let him put that in his pulpit pipe and preach it

I couldn't, could I, me, Adam Jones,
I couldn't preach Christ and him crucified,
Christ, I couldn't! Him, me, both of us dead or alive
In the manger-cradle, in the temple answering,
        Good Lord, answering the prelates.
        They're not worth it.
Christ on the cross, he would stick in my throat.
In or out of my throat, my mind, myself (whatever that is)
Would Christ be relevant and meaningful?
Why not preach me, unloved like any priest, and me crucified
Between the chancery office and the Vatican thieves,
All, all out to rob me of my identity,
Me, a priest, half and half a priest and not a man

All quiet on the priest front henceforth, now and forever?
I'm as jittery as the pope issuing his daily protocols.
Give me the edge on him, he doesn't know the underground
  is overground,
And him nosing around like a mole.
God save the king, long live the pope,
    Who cares for either? Not this unkinged king.
    Leave me alone.
    There was a time, the good old pre-Victorian days,
    Medieval people, they knew no better,
    Majesty did hedge the king or was it hedged the pope?
Am I naming Jones for king and pope and willynilly
Subsiding into the arms of a power structure?
    God go with me, a boy of a man,
    Defrocked, believing, disbelieving in priestianity,
        Discalced—I used to think that funny

Transcendent God, or sitting at the right hand of the Father,
What sense would that make rolling off my tongue?
With never a thought the old man could thunder it out.
Give us this day our daily bread of secular gods,
    They're plentiful as lice or mice or fleas, buzzing
  all around us,
    Drugs, sex, power, hate, hard cash,
I cannot preach them, either; piecemeal maybe
But not in rhetorical gobs and spouted dogmas,
And who needs them preached when everybody's
  worshiping them?
    Sermons, gods, men—
    Leave me alone

Yesterday, today, tomorrow
        Christ the same forever.
I'm no Christ. Yesterday *coram Deo et populo*
My maneuvers I guess you'd say were priestified,
A slumpiness, a show of half-ruthless unearned power,
A hail fellow well met triumphant scorn of people's
   joys and follies.
I'd found my happy home. Pretty much the priest,
        I could have posed at Hollywood
Now this day, what day is it? Good Friday, as if
   any day was good!
Today whether in the body or out of the body,
        St. Paul didn't know, did he,
        How could or should an ancient ex-scribe know?
        (And if out of the body what kind of "he" was he?)
Whether in or out of the priest-body, I do not know.
        Archangel Michael, could you apprise me?

I cannot damn my fix, much less goddam it,
And it ten times more me than any pertinacious fix.
Isn't there something about unloading your troubles
   on the stars,
And some lines, we had them in school, about the world,
   whatever that is,
        Too much with us, late and soon—
What is that piece? I'd rather be a pagan—
        Could any astrologer old or new, philosopher, magician
Up and tell us what a man would rather be?

# *Three Radio Sermons*

—1—

## Once Over Gently

Your youth and strength renewed like the eagle's
The Lord is a mighty God
The Lord is the Lord, over all,
The Lord is some one!
Our Ash Wednesday Communion Service
I invite you if at all possible,
open up our hearts that we may receive
what You are ready to give.
Proclamation of the Fatherhood of God, the theme
will continue with the kind of thing
God's kingdom in us should be.
Give us this day—around the tables of the rich
and the slums and the poorest cabins in the hills,
give us this day our daily bread.
Speaking of bread, the cheapest item
man can place on his table, the staff of life,
a universal food,
come and communicate with God on a daily basis.
Jesus had just begun to lay the base of his ministry
with, not only with those twelve but with all men.
Come to God daily and communicate with him,
sabbath to sabbath, crisis to crisis—
no, daily!

A parallel between payment of rent and our prayer:
if we don't pay, we are evicted.
When Jesus gave his disciples to pray this prayer
He was thinking back to the manna in the desert,
eat, if you store it up it will spoil.
Come to God daily with anything
with anything regardless
of how we consider its importance, with everything
and reconsider our whole scale of values,
the little things of life, our daily bread,
our interest in music or science
and the lowliness of life,
the little things, our daily bread.
This does not dishonor our Lord.
Our daily bread,
He took this little item, broke it and gave it

Naturally we will get our we's and me's mixed up,
the basic formula is for all people,
our daily bread, no hurt befall you,
go forth with the fellowship of all mankind.
Give me, Lord, my little self,
give me a social sense encounter
that Thy spirit may descend on those in high positions
as well as on us.
Be near to these people.
The Lord be with you till we meet again

—2—

## Amen Alleluia

I don't care how many people say there is no God
how many people say God is dead
let us thank the Lord, alleluia!
let the church say amen, alleluia!
Lord, that I have a fine automobile,
that He is the one can deliver you
that He is the one sets you free today
say amen alleluia!
All you that are able He said,
Come on to me and I will give you rest

Sit down and read the Bible, alleluia
God is good today, God has the power today
Let the church say amen, it's time to say alleluia
the Lord is with me, alleluia
you gonna get paid anyway
say you know God, alleluia

Stop your hippocrittin':
The same one created the universe, alleluia!
Let the Lord touch you today
let God be the one
don't try to do it yourself
God has all the power.
Hey, shut up, say alleluia
God sees you, He knows all things
Jesus heals my body today,
ask God to do something for you

I tell you to come out here
I guarantee God will deliver you
I want you to come out here, I want you in radioland
to set your hand on the radio
Lord God, stretch out your hand right now
and cure that asthma and that woman's got a stroke
Lord God, do it right now, pray heal him right now,
we thank you right now, alleluia!
Stop in and hear these men of God,
stop in and let God make you free

—3—

## From This Day On

From this day on I'll live for him
get an extry set, there's no record store anywheres near you
jus' turn to Jesus, you'll find a friend,
one to stick it closer than a brother.
The joy of serving the Lord on the wings of a dove,
from this day on my life begins
I want to walk in Jerusalem jus' like John
blest, healed and delivered by the power of God.
Until God's taken my hand,
I am tired, I am weak, I am old,
lead me, lead me, precious Lord.
From this day on I'm his, he's mine.
Take my hand, hear my cry,
lead me on, lead me home,

The living Lord is in them that believe on his name
don't miss out, don't miss out,
anywheres write that letter immediately
jus' to y'old neighbor, Box one, one, one
Do you know him? He is my everything
in the arms of my maker to stay
sheltered in the arms of God grace will lead me home.
I saw bones a-knittin', in a dream I did,
at the hospital I said, "Mack, I saw your bones a-knittin',"
let me tell you, folks, God is a great God
I am living on my hallelujah side!

You can imagine the sad situation—the bishop of his soul—
a sheep estrayed from its flock,
a-like humanity today and it's lost looking for security,

a man cannot conduct himself through this life,
cash, check or money order.
Rise up and walk: there's a cross for everyone to bear,
if you are still a lost sheep
be converted to the shepherd of your soul,
brother—brother or sister—turn to the Lord.
Remember Box one, one, one, a cross to share,
your letter postmarked before midnight Friday

To fill the world with love my whole life through,
now that you know what to do, to fill the world with love,
I hope to God there'll be enough Sundays left for you to repent
You are murdering us for convenience and profit
*Signed,* WLM, that's Women's Liberation Movement,
what do doctors use on their own women?
From this day on my sinful past it's all behind,
neighbor, where'll you find a bargain like that!
Along the way, wherever I go
I don't have to worry, He loves me so,
safe along the way He a-loves me so,
Teenager, NOW, NOW is very important
positive and powerful, bursting with hope
live with love and sex, encounter the realities of self,
confrontation, a materialistic society, you try love

To whom should I turn for the rest of the way?
God goes right down the line,
wonderful morn weary and worn
I don't have to worry, he a-loves me so.
Very nice pictures, "Where do we stand?"
Compact courses, back to the Bible
over forty of them, it tells you all in Bible courses
what's going to happen to Russia and Israel,
weary and worn he a-loves me so

## No God an Island

I am a Jew, but you papists and Baptists
don't you all have your fenced-in
cities of God and God's acres
        you all, we all
        ourselves, nosotros
Outsiders would undainty us
        ourselves, nosotros

Lord, keep us cozied up
no truck with the others' "Blessed be God"
"A Baptist was I bred and born
A Baptist will I die"
never let us scramble our praise with theirs

They're all right most of them
I suppose in their places
but it's by way of heavenly charism
that we're encapsulated here
others checked in over there
it is and ever more shall be so

Some of them now and then
might just chance to be
worshiping the bona fide God
you know within their lights and limitations
but for us to genuflect with them
        God forbid it
None of their idolatrous rigmarole
us and them praising God together

"Their idols teem, after them they run:
Shall I pour their blood libations? Not I!
Take their names on my lips? Never!
Yahweh, my heritage and my cup"

It's true, though, come to think of it
Jew, Moslem, papist, Baptist all solemnize:
        Holy, holy, holy
        Lord God of hosts
in riproaring campfire fashion
in papally approved or prayer-shawled huddle
the word desanctified if said together

Each alone-together speaks its piece
Jews alone-together, Moslems alone at sunset
papists alone, hardshell all alone
        each alone-together
        henceforth, now and forever

Suppose one cacophonous "Holy, holy."
Not yet, Lord!
We cannot do their alleluias
sing our songs in alien churches.
When and where they worship, that's okay
but ghosts dredged up from ages past
        say ourselves, nosotros
say to chant "no-no" forever
some imperious pope blurts "no"
a Jewish pope, a Southern Baptist
a tiaraed Roman pontiff:
        it must not be
        *verboten*
        *anathema sit*

Some time, somewhere, somehow
    hands across the sea
    *communicatio in sacris*
a deghettoized acclamation
we ourselves, nosotros
entering others' holy of holies
    once in a blue moon
    to live the living word
    with the familiars of God

## Me and God

*"In case you are not acquainted with him*
*as your personal savior." From a radio service.*

Me, Lord, merely me?
Lord, is there a merely cloistered me,
merely me and God,
me, just this whimpering me alongside God?
Could God reach out and save a lonesome desolate me,
me alone by my lank and naked self?
Is Jesus so bereft of company and partners
as to stand waiting to welcome only me,
is God that hard up?
Could I accept you, Lord Jesus,
as my personal and me-alone savior,
personally and privately my savior,
just me, this haggard nobody
occupying, monopolizing, shutting off the light
in a corner of your kingdom?

Two luminously self-evident beings in the universe,
God and himself—
So Newman, learned man and cardinal
reported that at age sixteen those were all he saw,
no third thus brightly shining.
What kind of uncommunity youthful saint was he,
blinded by me-and-God?
As for this me, I was never designed
by me and long-spun-out nature and the living God
To behold even darkly through a glass
so depopulated a community

### Unwashed

Littering up the streets, polluting the air,
it's people that litters up and pollutes!
Ever drive through the slums at night?
Scummy people, a giant vacuum cleaner
couldn't scour them off,
imagine their insides if they have any.
A hundred blocks across the city
too narrow a DMZ for me
why don't they build and own like us,
but who on God's green earth
is bustin' out to make room for them?

This Reverend Jackson's Operation Breadbasket—
where does he think our taxes go
besides wars and freedom for draft dodgers?
Grumbling, groveling, snapping
they're whelps, hungry bitches
lap up tons of relief and whine for more.
This Nader, he wants auto safety,
why not citizen safety—we pay for it!

New York with two million fat sleek bums
why don't you work I say to them
why don't you go and do likewise?
I've seen greasy ones in Dublin,
at Oxford on the steps of the Bodleian
old women shaking flowers at you in the rain
truncated arms, a leg or two sawed off
eyes like dirty lead-coated glass

*This poem appeared in the* U.S. Catholic

Find things to do, buy a home
it's simple on the installment plan
if they had Yankee git up and go,
budget like we do, send their kids to college.
What's to stop people that's got spunk?
Forty million, the "other America" some fellow said,
why didn't he say the shameless other half,
just say no red blood,
obscene blacks and Indians,
Chicanos and Puerto Ricans, gutless brands

Hate what is evil, hold to what is good—
that's old man Paul telling us
if there's anything red hot, get with it
that's what Paul (ever read him?) scribbled
in one of his squeamy letters.
But what's so precious in lopsided bags and paunches?
I'm a Bible buff myself, read it every day,
and when you throw a dinner invite the lame and
        crippled—
Show me though who does invite
the trash that never heard of ecology

## Whose Ox?

Sired by lily-white loins
was Beautiful
Begging with puppy for crumbs
was Beautiful
Damn-niggered and horse-whipped
was Beautiful
Justice and peace, mercy and truth some day to kiss
was Beautiful

Sneering at whitey, spewing obscenity
is Beautiful
Leapfrogging law and order
is Beautiful
Hope rising out of aristocratic rubble
is Beautiful
Asking what blacks are God-given to be
is incomparably Beautiful.

*This poem appeared in* Way

## Stand-Off

Because I never meet you face to face
in your hopes and fears and sufferings
never meet you in my parlor, at my table
never in your parlor, at your table,
never run and play, succeed and fail with you,
I and you don't, black and white,
Chinks and Yanks, Jews and Christians,
Christian and Christian, East and West, labor and owners

Because we never these two, three hundred years
a vacuum stands between us, a wall
as unscalable as that in Berlin or Jerusalem
where fraternizing is sudden death,
a hard-kept assumed superiority on either side

When people stand aloof from neighbor people
black and white, East and West and all the uptight echelons
when they see, but don't make friends at work or play,
suspicions crowd the man-made gap,
a world meant for love and sympathy
is occupied by bugbear guesses, major and minor wars
that drag on for a century or two
so that people cannot even be buried together,
the final schizophrenic stand-off

*This poem appeared in the* Ligourian

## And Merrily Go Round

What the world needs now is love
L-O-V-E, love and I mean it
Love, it makes the world go round
And merrily, merrily go round
And us drained of it, gaunt for it
Tell us not in mournful numbers
Love is but an empty dream

Love is life and life is love, Ashley Montagu says so
Put all your eggs in the love basket
A sanctiloquent and love-filled bishop says so
Love, says soft-sell Bishop Robinson,
Homes intuitively on the proper object
And I for one am glad he says so
And he a ringed and mitred bishop,
Authority sweetly spread all over him

I am glad the world's as simple as that,
My love homing rightly, eagerly and bishop-wise
On the proper object.
Don't sell me short, m'Lord Bishop,
Objects, objects, I'd liefer say
With due respect for precision and the cloth
Since my love homes on half a dozen girls,
Rightly and properly, the bishop said so,
Hierarchy with me all the long, long way from Peter

Loving is living, living and loving are one,
Copyright, Doctors Robinson and Montagu
I love, heaven knows I do, don't get me wrong
I'd give my life for any of my lovely loves,
Am with them, time to eternity
I love, alive, alive-O!

## How I Look

Frowzy dowdy me, I wouldn't
and couldn't let him peak at
the lines straight down nearly
from these two corners of my pouty mouth.
Why don't they go up and out,
can't I dammit iron them back?
There, back you devils, up and out
if I could just sponge into gay rivulets
this hippie hang-dog look in God's name!

Just touch up, brighten up you know
these two eyes, one, two and the pussycat chin.
Last night he whiskered my jowls
you know a little, roughed them up,
I'll have to say it was the wind flaking them.
Sir Galahad'll soon roll out of bed
and come to sweeten me up a teeny bit
this dingy minute when all of me points down

Nights, we say stilted words at God
routinish rounds thrown like bribes
you're up, we're down
is about the sum and size of it,
handy way to get lots off our chest
as we forgive—if we do—our debtors,

Ain't there some different procedure
things could day and night be done?
I wish if people just didn't have to work
but he says, he says I know how
maybe how to work and run things,
says I can start and get us off dead center.
If I wasn't so blasted tired this morning
and could remember: he said
it's initiate things I think he said
I can do and I guess orient them
more he says than he can—
a damn sight more, I'd say.
I wish if he'd just say it oftener,
for one spare word if he'd even once
I'd trade half my life, any half

Can't hardly ever budge out to anything
the way he jaws and lets go in traffic,
says his pocket's picked, thirty pieces missing,
you can't tote all the kids
or self-sitter them in the freezer,
and the way he looks women conscientiously up and down
measures their flabby, slabby round the middles
and me disembodied, a bare board

## God Be Our Witness

It just has to be, man,
enemies of the people get to acting up,
liquor gone straight to their heads
an occupational hazard,
seasons change, wheels turn and it's war,
it has to be

Callous to the point of obscenity,
feasting on the body count and defoliation
no knowing what they'd be up to next,
subterranean arms, high nuclear unrestraint
dragging bystanders reluctant
over the brink into hemispheral war
continents collapsing like a row of dominoes
God be our witness: our hands are clean

There's nothing like a peace-seeking war
to make a big man bigger
COSMOS stamped all over him
he cannot sit pantywaist by the kitchen stove
take blows of littleness on the chin,
half the world blazing away at war.
An affluent nation might have
to tomahawk aggression
wherever, this side of heaven,
its treacherous head bobs up

## Glut

Poor pretty little thing, the middle of her life
Saddled with four or is it five dirty babies!

Why don't the driver put her off, he has a right to,
Late middle twenties, can't be sure, God help us,
Pollutin' the countryside, herself and her screechin'
babies

All over the earth, and America blighted with the
stink of them
Maine to Oregon, down we go dead drunk under the
load of babies,
Global monitorin'—have I got that right?—
What's the use of it, no d-a-m-n good and us rotten
filthy, filthy—
Look at her smile, obscene, obscene,
Modern science wasted on her, never was through a
decent high school.
Cannot be herself, find her identity
Discover who she is, will never know who she is

One, two's enough, two plus a houseful
One and a half's the limit, the answer of science
Demographers, congress, HEW, medicos, all say so
How many dentists and we're already short on them
Dentists near collapse supplyin' teeth—how's your
—upper?—
How many dentists at five per, an infinity of dentists

*This poem appeared in the* Boston Pilot

Plenty short on dairy products, beef on the hoof,
hungry, hungry people
Too many babies, cut back the baby crop, stop the
obscenity
Too much corn on the cob, too many pigs on their
trotters
Cut, cut! Good Lord, right now I feel starved all over,
Me overweight? You're kiddin'
What's twenty, thirty? I'm starved to death.
The drove of them could do with corn and calves'
liver
Dentists you said, look, she's losing her teeth

Dirty! Pollutin'! Why don't she quick change the
diapers?
The pill they say is bad for cancer and all this blood
clottin',
But we found it's bad for diapers and we're in diapers.
Diaper business on its last legs, plant deodorized,
new-enterprized

A nation must act, down the drain with babies,
Sterilize, vasectomize, what does that puddin' face
know of
The facts of life, how to stop the jet of babies?

Pollutin' is mostly done by babies, they do the dirt
Our once free nation sunk in contamination, the air
we breathe,
Won't they stop it! Pray for air unpolluted
by babies.
HEW, it's official, says it's babies mostly do it
One and a half plus is your ration of pollutin' babies.
Decentivize the surplus crop, sock the co-creators
of babies

Think of Harlem, east part they say, but east or west
Think of all those dirty-dirty black babies
The air fetid with them, like confetti in attic and cellar

It's the end, it's the end of free America.
Babies start wars, that's proved, HEW said so
It's proved round and round the globe, get a law
        and stop them.
It's up to freedom-loving women
Stop war, fight back babies, halt this smog and pollution
Beget a law and stop these damn dirty babies

Dirty babies is half of it, the rest is cornfed baby
        beeves,
Stop the baby crop, stop the calves and corn,
Pity us starved, scrawny women, plump hind quarters,
Roly-poly like butter, our ribs sunk in fat, Lord stop
        the babies,
Perishing down we go, it's a national disaster
Get the congress, illegalize the spate of babies
Congress, D.C. judges say they'll pave the way,
Said stop wars, stop smog-pollution, stop the run
        of babies
It's all one thing, stop, stop, stop
        Babies, smog and wars coalesce and hang together

Don't we know, aint we sacrificed to death,
Don't I have a girl and she aint got no babies
Get an anti law, stop the corn and babies
We pray you Lord, D.C., right now
Stop the steaks and babies and this here pollution
A law to choke them off, baby-tax any daring to cross
The decency law and order line of one and a half plus,
Plus at most, slummites, farmerettes, black and white

We're dead set against discrimination
Rock 'em, sock 'em, a federal law's the thing

Lord, D.C., stop them now,
NOW'S the time
Save America the moral leader, don't let babies
submarine us
Save a free and famished people

They're pollutin', they're the pollutionist
animals
It's all gone rotten, rivers, creeks, parks and oceans
In Yellowstone itself did you ever see what the
black bears do?
The holiest earth we have, it's all gone rotten
Will there be a clean God's acre left to cremate us?
Shoulder to shoulder, not a cool breath of air
between us,
Look at Chicago smog-polluted, New York, upper
Michigan
Scads of big live bugs from the moon
Stop the corn and babies, my stomach's caving in

Kill the pigs, burn the corn, we can't rat-proof it
Pigs and corn they'd feed more lousy babies,
Too much food, we cannot feed the howling babies

Fallow farms and ranches baby-polluted all over
The hands of science tied, can't feed the babies
Everything wrapped up in super-technological
exploration
Can't find baby foods, water to wash the babies

Women in benighted early days
Fetched men a glut of babies
Slaves of men and lust, nothing to do but feed and
diaper,
Goose grease for their chests, oak and elm for coffins
Have to say they knew no better

Dear, dear politicos, no more trespassing babies
Get a law, a solid legitimized edict
Beseech the state and government to pre-evict latent
pregnancies
Put up a sign: Thus far, DMZ it, stop right now
Holy, holy, holy Lord God, D.C., we beg you flag it down
Saint HEW, you tell them: Stop it, one, two, no more
babies
Minus two the better side, the minus a plus for you,
Down the drain with babies
I thought we'd never see again this overflow
Ourselves driven to the wall with too much, too rich
victuals
Starved and polluted beyond redemption with corn
and babies

## A Package Deal

*Characters*

Dr. Eustace Egoutoir
Nurse Mollie Smothers
Nurse Susan Swansong

*Egoutoir:* *(precisely but choppily)* To the lab,
Sack them up, I said, bucket them off
*(ruminatingly)* Refuse, rubble,
Pollutants, high-grade, low-grade.

*Smothers:* *(solicitously)* This one here, Doctor,
Some of them squirm and twitch-like,
Good God, one yesterday I'll swear—

*Egoutoir:* The buckets, into plastic bags and buckets,
Incinerating stinks up the place *(sotto voce)*
A doctor's time, his life all tied up,
Busy man, his skill also, that counts. Don't stand there!
He's *bien engagé,* saving lives
And the public health, day and night.

*Smothers:* Right you are.

*Egoutoir:* Overworked men, no time for nambypambyism.

*Smothers:* That's right, Doctor.

*Egoutoir:* For all intents and purposes—
More salt, pre-sterilized like me—
They're what the profession calls dead,
Dead as a doornail when they hit the turf.

*Smothers:* I know.

*Egoutoir:* Indebted to science and the profession.
My advice to nurses: Get with it,
Get used to life, the way things are.
*(exits, the door slams).*

*This dramatic piece appeared in* Way, *April 1972*

*Smothers:* *(mopping up, trying to sing)* Buckets and bags,
Buckets and bags. I wish I could sing,
I used to sing, I liked to, day or night.
Buckets—today I cannot make it go,
Why can't I—just those two simple words
*(plumps into a chair)* Doc—he's off, singing,
I guess, to home
And at dinner *(slowly, thoughtfully)* the events of the day.
And if you give a dinner—
*(leaps to her feet)* Ye gods almighty,
if there are any gods almighty—
Oh God, my stomach! Hold everything!—
Be sure and invite the poor and lame
And the polluted, too, I guess.
The poor, they're stinkers, rat-racing for
hand-outs.
Hold! There it goes, pu-u-uke!
Who's a stinker, me, them, or my doc?
*(mopping up)* Buckets and bags, babies and—
Ba-abies and I said *(stomping)* pu-uke!
Going to—dammit what's wrong with the word,
A word's not dirty-pollutant.
God help or damn my polluted tummy
From here to eternity. What's in a stomach,
anyway,
But a lot of misplaced rumbling guts.
Wow, Mollie! There it blasts off again,
Twin pu-ukes, pu-ukety ukes!
It's up and out, an acidy, diaper stink,
Pollutant like dredged-up babies.
Doc though *(slowly)* doc he said they are not babies,
They're fetuses-pollutants—get with it.

*(Sitting down exhausted)*
Oh, my belly! He grunted that out: fe-tus-es.
Pol-lu-tants.
What's in a word, get used to life.
Babies are war-makers, too, he said, sure-fire,
Cluttering up housing and slums, crowding
The coming quality age off our panty-waist globe,
Quantity versus quality, can't say yet who'll win.
*(Enter Swansong)*

*Swansong:* What's all this fuss about?

*Smothers:* Quality, Susie, that's me and you. Babies is quantity.

*Swansong:* *(sniffing)* What do I smell—a rat? This place—

*Smothers:* *(swinging both arms)* Another swipe or two at pollutants,
We've got an Old Dutch hang-up on them.
A busy man, this doc. What's his Frenchy word
For it—*bean-a-gosh-a,* saving lives,
A man must, you know, get a move on,
Relieving terribly distraught mothers—
Mothers, mind you, Susie, but—

*Swansong:* I know.

*Smothers:* They are pregnant all over the lot,
Three, four a day, the doctors self-sacrificed,
Killed half to death, getting the baby rate
Down, live babies I mean, Susie,
Down to where it's at a standstill
Sorted and aborted right down to a zero pace.

*Swansong:* Did you, you Mollie, I mean you,
Did you personally ever have a fetus to unload?

*Smothers:* Winning, you know, Susie Susan,
Winning this here worldwide battle,
Too many babes in the undoctored woods,
The surplus baby crop, China, too, he says,
The Philippines and all of India
Or they'd run us people right off this planet,
And dirty black blacks—who says beautiful?—
He sure spews blacks out, spew!
Sure they cannot compete, can't pay a dirty
nickel.

*Swansong:* That's my doc, too, we land no black babies,
Black fetuses, dead or alive, smirking at you,
*(singing)*
Not me and my doc, me and my doc.

*Smothers:* You see, Susie, China, India, blacks,
They'd shove us people off the round earth.
He said we're winning the ancient battle
With starvation, too, though some
Of the women's paunches he punches,
They don't look over-starved to me,
Look, right here, Susie, at this spot,
One bitch was so stinking Chanel 5'd
I had to scour her fetid belly off.
Poverty, he said, Susie Susan, he said
It must be slimmed down or
Buttered up or something to where—

*Swansong:* Poverty, just wiggle the interest rates.

*Smothers:* A doctor's motives, he said, you know
Sure must be kept away up high,
A match for god-is-dead in the sky—
High and sky: I made a poem!

*Swansong:* Mollie kid, it's up to doctors and mothers,
It's their doing; and abortions, they're the in thing.
Who doesn't abort? Didn't you ever?
My doc, though, why does he double douse
His hands, the tips of his fingers? What's all so dirty
About a woman's non-liberated entrails
You know, to suction out an unwanted?
Were you, Mollie-O, among the great silent unwanted majority
Honest, now, were you an unwanted? Most folks are.

*Smothers:* Me? I sure do feel like it; my guts
Just now; that's what stinks.

*Swansong:* To the incinerator, down the drain with her,
Mollie, O Mollie, consigned to the ash can,
There's lots more where our Mollie came from.

*Smothers:* *(singing)* Buckets and bags, buckets and bags!

*Swansong:* Doctor, I say to him, here's the towel,
Not even a speck of blood. Damn the blood,
He says, why isn't it in the blood bank
Saving lives? There's lives to save!

*Smothers:* Accepting life, getting case-hardened.
Don't look at me like that, Susie Susan,
I'm okay, only *(slowly)* I know *(stops),* I know too much,
God, for a shot of primeval ignorance!
Squeak and squirm, but deadpan doc
Says to all intents and purposes
*(singing)* They're dead as rats and cats and elephants!

And this lousy world a damned sight
Better off, freer and cleaner
By about a million times. Pollutants,
War, poverty, hunger—that's what's
Got to go, aborted off the premises,
Bounced, got rid of henceforth, now
And forever, adieu dear filth!

*Swansong:* Unwanted pregnancies, God, Molly, they're thick as fleas,
The pill or something slipping.

*Smothers:* They happen—don't start to lecture me!
Cosmic accidents, acts of gone and goodbye gods.

*Swansong:* To cite my doc: If you only knew science
And de-mog-ra-phy—that's a jaw-breaker—
De-mog-ra-phy and the world situation,
Modern culture, he says his wife says, is in the balance,
Civilization itself, time is running out,
Civilization, he says she says, or what's left of it,
If you just knew what the world's all about,
The state law freely approved by the people, his wife said,
A man's got to do his thing and make a living.
I heard one vasected fellow talk, Mollie-O,
I thought he'd take his pants off right there,
He said God and man's salvation was in our hands.

*Smothers:* I guess it's keeping the wolf from the door.

*Swansong:* He said—

*Smothers:* *(doubling up in a chair)* What the hell do I care what he said!

*Swansong:* Me, neither. My doc he said
Doctors are high—highly bound
By oath to save the human race,
Formerly it was life, now it's the race,
It's nothing short of the race and mankind,
The modern drive for rights and freedom
To forestall this disaster overflow,
Blast it, he said, let's start here
And be free and pure for once on earth,
Poverty, God help nurses, it has no right to be.

*Smothers:* Suppose some day he rakes out twins,
Susie Susan,
It's double jeopardy, a twin killing.

*Swansong:* Don't make me sick, too

*Smothers:* Me, myself, namely Mollie Smothers,
Why was I ever born to be a baby-fetus nurse?
Baby blood goes round the clock with me,
Round and round, I see babies
In the coffee cup, impounded as in buckets,
Their flesh like the blasted gelatin we get,
Baby fingers in my cigarettes, I mean
Damned if I ain't abortion-soaked,
Seeing fetuses-pollutants all night long—

*Swansong:* Mollie! Keep your cool, Mollie, Mollie, Mollie!
You escaped the ash can, didn't you?
And who anyhow knows a fetus from a baby?

*Smothers:* What sort of god made this exploding madman world
Or who in hell did make it?
Did wanted and unwanted babies touch it off?
Can some lib man or depreciated woman tell me?

*(tapping her own head)*
Maybe, Susie, maybe I'm off my rocker,
Queasy, squeamish sick in the head,
*(singing to gestures)* Buckets and bags,
squeak, twitch,
Hit the turf, sudden death!

*Swansong:* Easy, girl, I said easy! Don't you think
A good half of the fetus doctors,
Can't we be sure their saline solutions
Roil their own m.d. guts? The money, though,
The money, Mollie, the money, King David
mansions
In California and Florida and trips
Around the medicated world.

*Smothers:* The money, I tell you!

*Swansong:* Honest to God some of them run ads,
Doctors and hospitals send underground flyers
To willing mamas. It's five, six hundred
Good solid, shake-me-down shekels
Prepaid in cash, that's legal, too.

*Smothers:* Cash, you know why.

*Swansong:* Sick of shekels, oh, no, I don't mean that.
But some are sick as hell of baby stuff, sick
I'll bet as your growling, grumbling stomach.
Are we, Moll, and our unattended rotund
bellies—
Here, Smothers, in the pit of my pit—
Are we the only ones with goulash dinners
Turned upside down? Though *(slowly,
thoughtfully)*
It's to save civilization and the world,
Mind you, don't forget, it's to save the world

*Smothers:* And civilization and things like that.
Stuff that mouth of yours, Susie! Don't talk, don't think,
For God's sake don't fall asleep and dream!
Susie, now listen, you barren bitch, listen.
This is how I dreamt all last night:
In my dream I was singing—don't laugh—
You know I used to sing.
A long, long way, ba-a-by (I sang),
You got to go *(singing),* via ditch and sewers,
A long way yet to the river,
A long slushy, slobbering way you've got
To go, to go unattended, ba-a-by—
*(changing to talk)*
No, he said I should say fetus-pollutant.

*Swansong:* Husha-by, baby.

*Smothers:* You know, he said it's to reduce
Soot and smog, dead fish and poisoned air and slums
And the world's hunger pains and poverty
And make all people safe for quality—
There you go: poverty and quality:
I'm a poet born of a dirty woman—
Six, seven hundred bucks a day
To keep the howling beast away.

*Swansong:* Poet you surely are.

*Smothers:* The dream, now you listen, Susie,
Said it was a long way yet to go,
Slimy pollutant, a long dirty way
To the capacious mother-breast of the sea,
Tossing, tossing on the sea—

*Swansong:* Cut it! Stop it! Your singing drives me nuts.

*Smothers:* *(singing)* Tossing on the sea, the sea, the sea,
Spinning—is that what baby-pollutants do?—
Spinning once, twice, three times
And coming back, baby mine,
Baby somebody's, if you hold together,
Pieces like chunks and slices of you,
Back around—glazed eyes stuck out—
If the pieces of you hold together.

*Swansong:* *(stopping Mollie's mouth)* For God's sake,
go easy I said,
It's getting you. A cup of jav, I wish it was
Whiskey ninety per cent proof, sip if you can
In a morgue. The other day my doc—
Oh, ain't he somebody, glamorous,
He could take any of us, any time—

*Smothers:* Could? Can? Does? Who is crazy
In this triangular two-some?

*Swansong:* Don't you love his nonchalant pose?
He said, I'll be damned if it ain't twins!
A package deal, two for one price!

*Smothers:* They'll turn up in my dreams as quints or quads.
Wasn't Freud himself scared of a death wish?
And how about our pets, the doctors,
Runty-grunty or glamorous as they come?
Did Freud ever get on the trail
Of unwilling mamas and unwanted babies
And things like the traumas we've seen?

*Swansong:* Now you're talking sense.

*Smothers:* Sense, girl? Listen! Back round the earth the
baby came—
Let me go on and tell it—
Back to zero-level-off the population.
Ba-a-a-bies, dirty things, who was it
Ever invented them *(half singing, half speaking).*

Am I on earth or walkie-talking
Hopefully I hope on the moon's far side,
Rocky slope and all. And the dream,
I couldn't stop it: are dreams for real?

*Swansong:* Shut up!

*Smothers:* It went on, it goes on, I cannot stop it:
Dirty, filthy babies, baby-pollutants,
Squirm, squeak, twitch!
Stop them, Mother of God, can't babies
Be switched off, choked, impeded or something?

*Swansong:* Silly! Just chuck the whole thing.

*Smothers:* Let me speak, Susan, worse, ten times worse
I saw:
Smog and smoke—shut up, let me go on.
What got me was the baby-fetuses living and
dead
Unhoused, unnamed, unclaimed
And doctor-pollutants, too, far-out doctors
disgorged,
I had never seen a doctor inside out,
Split down the middle from snorkel to saddle,
Doctors emptied out, playing dolls and
mud pies—

*Swansong:* Shut up, choke yourself!

*Smothers:* Retching fat voters' ribs, dessicated, empty
Oozy wombs, lots of them, vaginas
Hung on hooks—God, why can't I die, I said.
I actually prayed: Why can't a decent sick
man die,
Seeing all kinds of trash, people's trash,
Doctors' trashy trash, swill and slop,
Cigarette lungs grey as ashes,
Drugged and whiskied livers—

*Swansong:* Stop! You're going to stop! You're getting me!
*Smothers:* I saw a sow's lousy-looking ear
Like a ladle it was, or a jar I think
Half tipped over, or like a purse
Holding the fees for ousting pollutants,
How many fetus-pollutants to reach the brim?
Me a fool looking at filth and holding the forceps
Till my doc, the unglamorous grunter,
Was kidnapped *(Swansong winces)*—who says
*I'm* jumpy!—
That's what I saw—him held captive in Bolivia
Or off somewhere in the Andes of Spain,
The poor man's wife cashing a year's abortion
salary—
Take it easy, you! Don't shake all over—
Himself a sterilized heroic un-father.
*Swansong:* You're crazy, Moll, to go rehashing all that stuff.
Of course, babies and things like that happen,
They're pollutants preventing quality,
Didn't your kidnapped runty-grunty
Scientifically tell you so? Don't crack up!
*Smothers:* I half-wish I could go just plain mad
And they'd bucket and bag me off
Like a whimpering baby-pollutant.
The dream, it was broken and then
Hung together again and I was saying:
"Those twins, Doctor, were they boys or"—
And he said, "Who the hell cares now?"
And I asked him once—am I dreaming it,
Susie?—I asked him did he think
The live ones would grow up lovers.
*Swansong:* Lovers? Don't say love!

*Smothers:* You know, like us and other people,
And they'd float gaily around the world
And come back maybe collared
Round their necks with unpolluted flotsam.
Sing it with me, sing Susie:
Buckets and bags, buckets and bags!
Couldn't I here—what's wrong, Susie?
Couldn't Mollie Smothers take a little global jump
Unattended, half-way out of here—

*Swansong:* For God's sake, I said—*(collapsing)*

## Three Birds

Dr. Rock he made a pill
And all the women took it
He stuck a feather in his hat
And called it anti-ovit
All it's good for, the doctor said,
Is to hold up ovulation
This insistent-persistent ovulation
To keep the egg from sinking,
For me, it's science and love of the game
Simply by way of experimentation

But said the women, for the distaff
It's a hunk of amelioration
Yea boy this is a freedom proclamation,
For the first time women's equalization
And look sharp, woman said to woman and girl to girl,
If it does, and the doctor said so,
If it does, if it holds up there'll be no babies this here moon
There'll be a complete drop-out of babyfication

Bring yourself well pilled to school, said teacher,
Along with pencil and paper
For who can tell how brave and strong the pretty little girls'
The pretty little girls' flirtation
Who can say how depth-unmanning the boys'
The big boys' gluey-eyed fascination
The girl foams up, she never foams down
That's the good of it: no baby fall-out
No chancy baby co-creation

And that's not the half of it,
Reformers, politicos and preachers said,
It could stop, put a quick dead stop to this pop—
This pop—this business of population,
It could chill, it could kill whatever it is
That causes population,
And much better, surer they said in chorus
Than oldtime incantation

That's bird two and look at three:
With the same swift blow
Remove, renege, revoke, what you will
The wide world's thick pol—
This pol—the whole wide world's pol—pollution

## Any Rags, Any Bones

—1—

Schweitzer, philosopher and medicine man—
did you ever by the grace of God
see him, hear him, heroic on any count
medallioned by academies
but opting for the jungle
the word he spoke: Let life be!

Old, decrepit, creaky legs to stand on
who am I to side with God and Schweitzer
to say or unsay life and death?
God (I'm glad to announce)
made me, as life itself, pro-life.
So what is new in Paul or John?
Who is scandalized, incensed
and I am not on fire
a stumbling, mumbling blockhead
letting go with God and Schweitzer

—2—

The race well stocked with life pellets,
for God's and life's sake desist
London and New York dead broke
Rome, Shanghai pressed down
        running over
        let's let blood!

Teens carrying a premature load,
can't we trimester babies into oblivion?

*This poem appeared in* Way, *Jan.–Feb., 1977*

Medicos, life-protectors
lovers of life
spare our girls this unpleasantness
spare society low-quality, nuisance people

The life-globe doused with pre-persons
court delivered
unnamed, unpitied, unloved
mini persons like you and me
like Einstein, Assisi, Shakespeare
three cut out for superstars

—3—

Dorothy Day gambling on faith
in the plenteous commodity "life"
picking up broken pieces of persons
is better with our multiplying species
than abortionists from Albany to Frisco
Dorothy's running mate
Teresa of Calcutta
her pockets inside out
scavenger of life
baby life, old people's lives,
Bangladesh discards,
any rags, any bones, any bottles today?

Dorothy and Teresa, help us
to believe in God the Father Almighty
Creator of life on earth and in heaven
in resurrected life
in the life-giving Spirit
the confession of sins
and life everlasting. Amen.

## A Minor God

—1—

Philosopher George Herbert Mead speaking:
Don't be quashed as submissive *me,*
Fight it out as the *I* you are.
Pascal demurring:
Man essentially a lie and a liar
Making the I-me the center of the universe

—2—

I do, you and all do
That's our decent man-shape way
Things converging on me, I know them.
Higglepiggledy, no heads or tails they come
I make them known things, make them be me
Bring into my orbit things of earth and sun and moon
Relocate them, build them into my impoverishment
Make them consubstantial with me
Domesticated within my ecology.
A hat is on my head, a car is mine at the door,
Things known turn into the I-me of my self

—3—

Resentful of our being the gods we are
Pascal did not want the world the way it is,
I make things of nature and the secrets of God
Kneel to me, be in me, by me
Intellect a thief of all things
and love wedding us happily to all

—4—

Not that the I-me is a safe repository,
I forget and my purloined world falls apart
Disintegrated, gone with the wind,
A hairline moment and part of the I-me
Is gone forever

—5—

"Dissolving in the chemic vat
Of time, man, gristle and fat"—
What to do at that point?
The poet Kunitz proceeds: Man
"Lifts his impermanent face to watch the stars"
The mind free to move everywhere
Disdainful of time and space
Tied to them with trees and ants
And running through worlds unbound.
Royce: the mind knows
That it knows that it knows.
Aquinas: the present act of knowing
Grasps the present act of knowing.
By leave of Royce-Aquinas, that is something
Of the I-me in me, of me, by me

—6—

Struggling and loving to be, the I-me is comforted:
*Non omnis moriar*—something of the I-me will be
Though looking like a plaster god that falls apart.
Not wholly, said Horace the poet,
Not wholly, said the philosopher, a spark, the tiniest bit,
The alivest particle invincible,
The co-creator part of I-me
Stands impassible, impervious,
Bound down today, inexpressive,

Tomorrow freed from limiting encasement, it shows
What the I-me
Eternally is,
Unsubjected to chance and tranquillizers,
Emancipated from all that leaves indentation,
It is *Athanaton kai aidion*
Its life style changed, lifeful everlasting

—7—

Now at last more freed
Than Keats on first looking into Chapman's Homer,
A lone watcher of the skies
Blinded by new patches of stars,
More freed than Balboa and his men staring at the Pacific
The freed I-me
Beyond Homer, Chapman, Keats and the Pacific,
These the polyphony of nothing

—8—

The Israelites come back home
To their hearths and themselves
Then were like men dreaming, their souls new-born
Filled with joy and laughter.
The I-me freed, itself next to God,
Said Alexander the Aphrodite,
The I-me identical with God,
Its intuitions and love-knowledge, said Averroes,
The thought-life of God
The I-me more illumined than at the unrecorded moment
When it first saw that I am I and
Eternally am an inviolable I

—9—

The present compound amalgamated me,
The spark of God-thinking in me,
Is too much with me, fenced off from other me's,
Black me's, Jew and Hindu me's, DP me's
Strangers condescended to,
Not half way up to the I-me mighty throne,
This solemn and lonely god

## Walking on the Moon

Walking on the moon, we now find
        Said deluxe scientist, Glenn T. Seaborg,
        Is not for sure walking in God's shoes,
        Not shoving pie-in-the-sky over the cliff
                Into primeval chaos
To make room for preferred gods and goddesses,
A pantheon competing,
        complying, already triumphant

Commuting between earth and moon
Resplendent in our risen robes
        Makes our seamy side look all the seamier,
        Makes us feel ourselves the same old dingdong people
        Slugging it out day and night in the streets
        Chunks of us left good as dead,
        The rest poised picador for interplanetary war
        And always belligerent
        Round our monotonous hometown globe

*Winner of the Laus tibi Deo poetry award, 1971*

Too proud, too affluent to admit we cannot win
With only fifty, sixty thousand killed
versus
Six hundred thousand dead of our beloved enemy
plus
10 × 600,000 maimed, defoliated
Too dazed to ask whether "we cannot win" means
The invincible we have lost a war
The draw a belly-blow to Uncle Sam.
Walking on the moon, said Seaborg,
Prime minister for Atomic Energy,
Is walking on rocks,
Not on streets of pearl and gold,
Upsets our ecological balance,
Teeters us toward hubris,
Our alleluias mixed with doubts and queries

Science, Seaborg surely meant to say,
An immeasurable value, is goal and end.
It's what super-animals are destined for,
Equipped by evolution, God and man
To full fathom the moon's rock culture,
Stub our toes on corrugated Jupiter,
Land face up on the North Star,
Transport lungs intact
from
Buenos Aires
to
Johannesburg,
Trade a liver, bargain for a heart.
And yet this man Seaborg, scientist, holding back
kept skeptically wondering whether
In unaffluent, unarmed simplicity
The Jobs and Socrates distance us as wisdom hunters

## Ultimatum

Don't you think as an ultimatum
The race, black, white and brown
Could do with, stands in need of, hankers for
Emancipation
To say little or nothing of some evangelist's or two's
Sure-fire quick salvation